BRITAIN in VICTORIAN TIMES

LIFE IN BRITAIN

KU-328-704

Contents

4 An Age of Progress

6 Inventions

8 Transport

10 Factory and Office Work

12 The Lower Class

14 The Suburbs

16 Life in a Great House

18 Schools

20 Leisure and Entertainment

22 Health and Hospitals

24 Church and Chapel

26 Clothing and Fashion

28 After the Victorians

30 Timeline

30 Places to Visit

31 Glossary

31 Books and Websites

32 Index

An Age of Progress

The Victorian age lasted through the reign of Queen Victoria, from 1837 to 1901. During this period, life changed faster than it had ever done. It was an age of many new inventions and ideas.

The population of Britain increased by a half, and many people moved from the countryside into the towns and cities. Britain became the first modern industrial country, with railways providing efficient transport and large factories making goods of every kind.

Some small towns, such as Glasgow, Manchester and Birmingham, grew into great new cities. City streets became more and more crowded with horses, carts, trams and bicycles. New rows of workers' houses covered areas of countryside, and soon became black and ugly with smoke from the factories. The workers were poor, but the factories made the cities rich. Some factory owners gave money to help make Victorian city centres attractive places, with new hospitals, schools, museums, parks, town halls, railway stations and libraries.

▶Many of the industrial areas, such as South Wales and northern England, grew around coal mines. The coal provided power for steam-driven machinery.

Major
◦ industrial towns
■ Industrial areas
▬ Coalfields

Glasgow

Newcastle

Bradford
Bolton
Wigan
Leeds
Manchester

Birmingham

▶ The world map on this souvenir plate, made to celebrate Queen Victoria's Golden Jubilee in 1887, shows the British Empire coloured red. It covered over a fifth of the land surface of the world.

Country life

In the countryside life changed more slowly. More people worked on the land in Victorian times than now. There were no tractors. Most tasks were done by hand or, for jobs like ploughing, using a horse.

Social classes

In the Victorian age, people's lifestyles depended on their wealth and also on their **social class**. The richest were the **upper class**, who owned large houses, did not need to work and had many servants. The **middle class** had comfortable lives, but usually the man of the family worked, often in an office. Most people belonged to the **lower class**, many of whom were very poor indeed. Those who had jobs worked in factories, on farms or as servants.

▼ The Great Exhibition opened in London in 1851 to show off the wonderful inventions and products of Britain and the Empire. It was held in a glass and iron building called the Crystal Palace. The exhibition lasted 141 days; six million people came to see it.

The British Empire

Britain built up a huge empire, which included India, Canada, Australia, New Zealand and many parts of Africa. From those countries **raw materials**, such as cotton and metal ores, poured into Britain. Here they were processed into more expensive products like fabrics and machinery, which were then sold on for a profit.

Inventions

The 19th century saw great changes in science. Many of the things we use today, such as telephones, sewing machines, electric light bulbs and cars, were invented in the Victorian period.

The first photographs were taken in the 1830s. Within a few years, most towns had a photographic studio. Here families went in their best clothes, to have their picture taken. They had to stand still for a long time, otherwise the picture would be blurred. Smaller cameras that could be carried around were invented later, making it easier to take snaps of outdoor scenes.

▲Family photographs were often mounted in special albums. It was not possible to take colour photographs so albums often had extra decorations, such as these flowers – from a Victorian album in Brodsworth Hall, South Yorkshire.

THE PENNY POST

Before 1840 letters were seldom posted. This was because you did not pay when you sent a letter but had to pay when you received it. This could be very expensive if you lived a long way from the sender. A retired teacher called Rowland Hill persuaded the government that more people would send letters if a fee was paid at the time of posting. In 1840 his idea became the Penny Post. People could send a letter to any address in the country by sticking a penny stamp on it.

Steel

In 1854 Henry Bessemer found a way to convert iron into steel, which was both stronger and lighter than iron. This made it possible to build huge structures such as the Forth Railway Bridge in Scotland and the Tamar Bridge near Plymouth. Ocean-going ships, made of steel rather than wood, became larger and larger. Railways were re-laid with new steel rails.

Steam power

New uses were found for inventions that had been made before the Victorian age. One of the most important was the steam engine, which powered factory machinery, ships and trains. By the 1880s steam power was also being used to turn dynamos in power stations in order to make electricity.

Electric light

After the invention of the light bulb in the late 1870s, electric light started to replace the dim, yellow gas light, oil lamps and candle light. Some town streets were lit by electricity too, making them more welcoming at night.

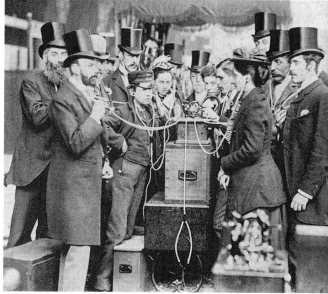

▲These people, visiting an exhibition in London in 1892, are listening to a phonograph. This an early form of record player. Today it would sound very scratchy compared to our CD players.

▼When it was opened in 1890, the Forth Railway Bridge was one of the largest bridges in the world. It crossed a huge river and made train journeys to northern Scotland much faster.

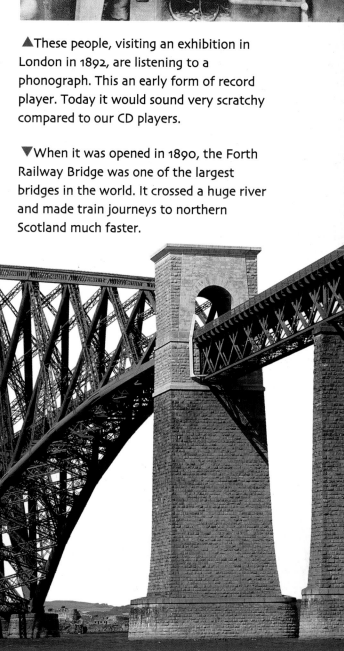

Transport

During the Victorian age new forms of transport allowed more and more people to travel. Food had to be brought in from the countryside for the growing towns and cities, and materials transported to and from the factories.

The biggest change was the building of the railways. The first steam trains had appeared shortly before Victoria's reign. But in the 1840s and early 1850s private companies built 13,000 kilometres (8,000 miles) of railways all over Britain. Trains were much faster and cheaper than canal boats or horse-drawn carriages.

At first some people were frightened by the idea of railways, believing the high speeds were dangerous. Sometimes passengers were killed when they tried to get off while the train was still moving.

▼ A painting by W P Frith showing a busy scene at Paddington Station, London, in 1853. Luggage is loaded onto the top of the train. Passengers travelled first, second or third class. The well-dressed ladies on the right can probably afford to travel first class. Third-class travel on the earliest railways was in open trucks.

▶ The first cars appeared in late Victorian times, but only rich people could afford them. Early car drivers were required to have a special attendant walking in front of the car, holding a red flag as a warning. These drivers were photographed in Brighton in 1896.

BICYCLES

Bicycles became popular in the 1870s. The penny-farthing, or 'ordinary', had one big wheel and one small wheel. The tyres were solid and very hard. The penny-farthing was used mostly by the wealthy for fun. In 1885 the 'safety bicycle' was invented. It was the first bicycle that had gears and chains. People began to cycle to work. By the 1890s about a million people belonged to cycling clubs. Club members rode together on day-long outings into the countryside.

THE CYCLE PARADE MARCH

by THEO: BONHEUR.

LONDON; W. PAXTON 19 OXFORD STREET. W.

1089 *

Steam was also used to power great iron steamships that crossed the ocean faster than ever before. Many people left Britain, sailing away to start a new life in Canada or Australia.

Journeys across the city
Short journeys were often made by a horse-drawn carriage known as a hansom cab. This was like a taxi: it could be stopped in the street, and went wherever the passenger wanted to go.

A cheaper way of travelling in the city was to take an **omnibus** ('bus' for short) or a tram. The tram's wheels ran along metal slots in the street. The early buses and trams were horse-drawn, but later ones were powered by steam, then electricity, and then petrol. The upstairs had no roof, and was called 'outside', while downstairs was 'inside'.

◀ This cover for some printed music shows both men and women cycling. Women soon found that their long skirts got caught in the wheels, so they began to wear 'bloomers' – like very baggy trousers – that were more practical.

Factory and Office Work

There was plenty of work to do in Victorian times, but much of it was boring, dangerous and poorly paid.

In the new industrial towns such as Manchester and Birmingham, many people, including children, worked in factories. Many worked in **textile mills** that made cloth and thread from wool, cotton and silk. Other people did 'outwork' at home, such as making brushes or gloves, sewing dresses or spinning thread. They were often paid even less than factory workers.

Obeying the rules

Factories had very strict rules. You could be fined for wasting materials, arriving dirty or late, chatting or even singing. Factories were dangerous and noisy, and workers who were injured or fell ill did not get paid for time off. Children were made to clean machines while the machines were kept running, and there were many accidents.

◀Manningham Mills was a silk mill in Bradford. The huge chimney allowed the smoke from the steam engines to escape. The owner was proud of his factory. He built it in a grand style because he wanted it to look impressive.

Later, laws made working hours shorter, and owners of textile mills (but not, at first, owners of other factories) were required to put guards over parts of machines to make them safer.

Clerks and typists

In the mid-19th century few lower-class people could read and write well. Those who could might get a better-paid job as a clerk or office worker, in a bank or company office. Clerks often sat on tall stools, at sloping desks that made it easier to write. Because there were no photocopiers then, some clerks spent all day copying documents by hand, writing with a pen that they dipped in a pot of ink.

▲ Weavers in a Lancashire cotton mill in the 1890s. Men were paid just about enough to cover rent and food, but women earned half a man's wage and children even less.

Later in the Victorian period, typewriters were invented. Typing was considered a suitable job for women and gave many the chance to work in better-paid office jobs. As a result, the number of women working in offices increased from just 7,000 in 1881 to 90,000 in 1901.

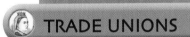

TRADE UNIONS

Some workers organised themselves into groups called **trade unions** to try to get more money and improve their working conditions. Many factory owners hated the trade unions. Later in the Victorian period, as trade unions became more powerful, factory owners realised they would have to listen to them.

◀ The Bermondsey branch of the National Union of Railwaymen, photographed around 1900. Trade unions had special banners and drums that they used when marching through the streets. Their marches showed everyone that they had many supporters.

The Lower Class

The lower class was the poorest part of the population. In Victorian times it was also the largest. It included factory workers, farm labourers and those with no job at all.

Most lower-class people rented houses, flats or just a room from landlords. Factory owners built many cheap homes for workers, close to the factories. In northern England rows of houses were sometimes built 'back to back', with no gardens between. In Scottish cities like Glasgow many lived in tenements (blocks of flats).

▶ Saltaire, near Bradford, was a factory village built by a kind factory owner who wanted his workers to live in a healthy, clean place. The houses were much better constructed than most in Bradford.

◀ So that workers' houses could be built as cheaply and quickly as possible, they were constructed in long rows (or terraces) like these in Leeds. Bricks for building were brought into the cities by the new railways.

THE WORKHOUSE

There were no pensions or benefits from the government to help very poor people who were unemployed, or too old or sick to work. They might get a bed and food in the local or parish workhouse. But these were harsh places. Inmates had to wear uniform, and the unemployed were given hard, boring work to do like removing tar from ships' ropes.

▲Women eating a meal in St Pancras workhouse, London, in 1895. In the workhouse, husbands and wives, and parents and children, were separated from each other. The workhouses kept people alive, but nearly everyone dreaded having to live in one of them.

Poor people could not often afford meat, but ate cheaper food like potatoes, bread and cheese. There were rarely carpets, curtains or wallpaper in their homes, and the furniture was simple. But people might have one or two luxuries, like a picture or a china ornament.

A very poor family might have to live in one noisy room. Rubbish was often just thrown out into the street. Diseases like cholera, typhoid and smallpox spread in these dirty conditions and killed many people.

Farm workers' cottages

Country people usually lived longer than those in the cities. This was partly because the air was much cleaner, and partly because they ate better food that they grew themselves. Most kept a pig which was later killed for food. But farm workers' families often had to live in cramped cottages of one or two rooms rented from the farmer.

Improvement and reform

Later on in Victorian times, living conditions improved for the lower class. Local councils were allowed to pull down unhealthy **slums**, which were replaced by better houses. **Sewers** were built under city streets, to take away toilet waste and dirty water from every building. Clean water was brought to houses through lead pipes.

The Suburbs

As the industrial cities grew, their centres became very noisy, smoky, dirty and crowded. Many better-off people went to live in new suburbs, built outside the centre but joined on to the rest of the city by the new railways and other forms of transport.

Suburbs were quiet and pleasant areas to live, with wide streets and plenty of trees. If you were wealthy you might live in a detached house, which stood separately from its neighbours and had a large garden. Many Victorian suburban houses had bay windows, which stuck out so that rooms had more daylight.

Commuters

From the suburbs, many men travelled into city centres to work, perhaps to an office. Most went by tram, train or bus. Many suburban railway lines were built for **commuting**. In London the Underground opened in 1863.

▲ Middle-class families often lived in semi-detached houses like this pair in Putney, a suburb of London. Today families still live in these houses but very few have servants.

▶ The first carriages on the London Underground had no roofs, and travel must have been very uncomfortable. But soon the Underground became a popular way to commute from the suburbs.

As these lines opened, more and more suburbs were built. Villages like Wimbledon and Brixton became suburbs of London, while new suburbs appeared around many other cities, including Birmingham, Manchester and Glasgow.

Life for the middle class

The people who lived in the suburbs were mostly from the middle class. Unlike the upper classes, the man of the family usually had to work, but they had enough money for luxuries like good clothes. They were very proud of their houses, and spent a lot of time keeping them clean and tidy. Most middle-class families usually had at least one servant, who would live at the top of the house. In general, middle-class women did not have jobs.

Before Victoria's reign, rich and poor people often lived close to each other in villages or small towns. But now, living in a suburb might mean that a middle-class person hardly ever saw a poor person in their neighbourhood.

▼ The sitting room in a Victorian middle-class house was usually cosy but rather cluttered. There were armchairs, wallpaper, potted ferns, carpets, lots of pictures, and perhaps a large mirror over the fireplace.

Life in a Great House

The richest people in Victorian times were the nobility (people with titles like Lord and Lady) and others who owned a lot of land, and wealthy factory owners. They often lived in grand houses in the countryside, with large gardens around them.

The owners of the house often had friends to stay for house-parties that might include fox-hunting and shooting pheasant and grouse.

The servants

All the work in the house was done by servants. Many servants were from poor families in the country. They were paid little and had to work long hours. But to many of them this was a good job, with somewhere to live, and food and smart uniforms provided.

◀The billiard room in Osborne House, Queen Victoria's home on the Isle of Wight. Grand houses had impressive rooms, splendid staircases and often a ballroom for dances.

WHAT WAS THE EVENING MEAL LIKE?

Evening meals were often very long, with soup, fish, chicken and beef, as well as a choice of puddings like jelly and ice cream. It was not considered ladylike for women to eat big meals. If they were hungry, sometimes they ate in their rooms, then came down to join the others and delicately picked at their food. After the meal, the men went into the billiard room, smoked cigars and talked about politics or business. The ladies went into the drawing room, perhaps to play cards.

The butler was the head of the servants. He opened the front door to visitors, who would give him their visiting card with their name on. He took it to the master or mistress of the house, who would then decide whether or not to see the visitor.

There were also gardeners and gamekeepers to work in the grounds, housemaids to clean the rooms, and footmen to carry things and do other heavy work. The lady of the house often had a lady's maid, who looked after her clothes and arranged her hair.

▲ The dining room in Brodsworth Hall, South Yorkshire. The family of the house ate at a long table lit by candles. Children ate separately with their nanny in the nursery.

▶ The restored kitchen at Brodsworth Hall. The cook was in charge of the kitchen, which was on the ground floor of the house. Kitchen and scullery maids helped out, by cleaning pans, washing up and chopping vegetables.

Schools

A Victorian school was often a rather stern place. Classes tended to be large, and lessons serious. Pupils copied words and sums, using a thin, pencil-shaped piece of slate that made white marks on a large, flat slate, which they could later wipe clean. Often the teacher made the class learn poems by heart, or read out passages from books such as the Bible.

Children from well-off families often learned how to read and write at home from a **governess** (woman teacher) or a male tutor. Later on, parents would send their sons to a boarding school, where they lived for a whole term at a time, and studied classics (Greek and Latin). Older middle-class boys might go, as day pupils, to a grammar school. As there were few girls' schools, daughters usually continued with the governess, learning subjects like French, music and needlework.

▼ The Bonner Street Board School was built for poor children in Hackney, London, in 1875. In large schools boys and girls were often in different classes, although each class might have children of widely different ages.

Poorer children

Life was very different for children of poorer parents. In early Victorian times, many did not go to school at all, because schools were not free and there was no law saying children had to attend. Some children went to dame schools (classes taught by a woman in her own home).

▲ Dinnertime at a London Ragged School in 1869. Ragged Schools were free schools run by charities for orphans and the poor, who were glad to get a free lunch. Most of the teachers were older pupils called monitors.

Changes in the law

From 1870 schools were provided for all children aged 5 to 10, but their parents had to pay for their education. Poor families could hardly afford it, but they risked being fined if they did not obey the law. By 1891 schools were free, and from 1899 all children had to stay at school until they were 12.

▼ These young Lancashire girls, photographed around 1900, spent Monday to Saturday hard at work in a noisy factory. Most of them would have left school at the age of 12.

CHILDREN WHO HAD TO WORK

In early Victorian times many young children had to work to earn money for their families. Some children worked as chimney sweeps, climbing narrow, sooty chimneys to clean them. Others worked in coal mines, opening and shutting trap doors to let wagons through, or else cleaned machines in factories. Others did odd jobs like selling matches, sweeping the road or scaring birds in farmers' fields. Slowly the government passed laws banning children from working in dangerous places like factories and mines.

Leisure and Entertainment

Without television or radio, people in Victorian times spent much of their leisure time at home making their own entertainment.

Families might listen to mother or father reading the latest Charles Dickens novel, or a daughter playing the piano. Or they else they enjoyed a game of charades, cards, chess or dominoes. Many women sewed clothes, or embroidered as a hobby.

▲ Toys like these building bricks would have been quite expensive. They probably belonged to middle-class or upper-class children.

Theatre and music hall

Men and women often went out together to the theatre. Those who were rich went upstairs to sit in the dress circle. Many lower-class and middle-class people enjoyed going to the music hall. This was a theatre where the audience often sang along with the performers. Sometimes there were jugglers or comedy acts, too. Famous music hall songs were very popular and often sung in pubs.

Strolling in the park

On Sundays city people often relaxed by going to a park. Because many people lived in cramped homes and worked in dark, noisy factories, new city parks were created to provide clean air and space. There were lakes for boating on, and bandstand concerts. Some rich factory owners opened public parks for their workers.

Holidays

In early Victorian times people worked six days a week, with Sunday off. The only other holidays were Good Friday and Christmas Day. The first Bank Holidays were introduced in 1871. By 1900 many people had the time and money to take holidays away from home.

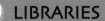

LIBRARIES

Some Victorian politicians felt strongly that books and learning should be available to everyone. In 1850 a law was passed allowing towns to spend public money on building public libraries, with free membership for all. Victorian libraries were in grand rooms with notices saying 'silence'. Often you had to ask for the book you wanted rather than choosing one yourself.

A day at the seaside

Many people went to the seaside for a holiday. At first only the well-off could afford this, but the railways made it quicker and cheaper to get to the coast.

◀A cricket match at Lords in 1892. Playing and watching sports like cricket and football were popular in Victorian times. In 1872 the first football FA Cup final took place, and around the same time the modern forms of tennis and rugby union were introduced.

▶Holiday-makers on Margate pier, 1897. Towns such as Margate, Blackpool and Llandudno became popular seaside resorts. There were Punch and Judy puppet shows on the beach, and long iron piers where everyone strolled.

Health and Hospitals

In the overcrowded towns and cities of Victorian Britain, diseases passed from one person to another very quickly. Most families were large and expected that one or two children would die young.

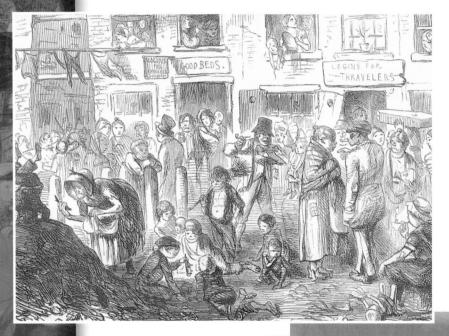

People were very frightened of falling ill. Those who had money would pay a doctor to treat them at home. Many people tried to cure themselves. There were plenty of ready-made medicines on sale, but most didn't do what they promised.

▲In dirty, crowded slums like these of the 1850s, diseases such as cholera, caught from drinking polluted water, spread quickly and killed many people, young and old. By 1900, just 25 years after the Public Health Act of 1875, cholera had disappeared in Britain.

IMPROVING PUBLIC HEALTH

A series of laws were passed in Victorian times to make homes and cities healthier places. One of the most successful was the Public Health Act of 1875, which allowed town councils to buy up and demolish poor-quality slums that were a risk to health. New houses had to be much better built, with windows in every room and good drains. Many homes began to have flush toilets, clean water and better ventilation.

Early hospitals

In early Victorian times, hospitals were dirty, crowded places and were used mostly by the poor. Nurses knew hardly anything about medicine, and there was very little equipment. During the Crimean War (1854-56), a nurse called Florence Nightingale was horrified by the bad conditions in the military hospitals and worked hard to improve them. In 1860 she opened the Nightingale School of Nursing in London.

▲Medical students watch surgeons at work in Charing Cross Hospital, London, 1900. Before 1840 patients having operations were conscious as the doctors cut their bodies open. By the time this photograph was taken, anaesthetics had been invented that put patients to sleep so they would not feel anything.

This was the first hospital to train women to become nurses. Gradually hospitals improved, with space between the beds, and well-trained nurses in clean uniforms.

The big clean-up

At first no one realised how important cleanliness was in preventing the spread of germs. But in 1871 an antiseptic spray was invented that killed germs and stopped infections. By the end of Victoria's reign much more was known about curing illnesses and how necessary it was for people, hospitals and homes to be hygienic. As a result of the changes that were introduced, people began to live longer.

Church and Chapel

Christianity was the main religion in Victorian Britain, as it is now, but more people went to church in Victorian times. Many families went to Church of England (Anglican) services every Sunday.

In the new factory towns, however, there were few churches for workers to go to. Many workers also thought that the church was only for the rich. Since Sunday was their only day off, some of them preferred to stay at home and rest.

Different types of Christianity

Some poorer people belonged to other Christian groups, such as the Methodists and the Baptists. They worshipped in plain, simple **chapels** rather than churches. They opposed gambling and the drinking of alcohol. Many Irish workers, who had moved to Britain to help build the railways and canals, were Catholics.

Charity work and social clubs

The churches helped the poor of the industrial cities by setting up new churches and charities. Church social clubs were meeting places where people could drink cocoa instead of spending too much money on beer or gin in the pub.

◀ This picture, painted about 1880, shows a girl, her mother and her grandfather sitting on a church pew. Ladies wore hats in church, but men removed theirs.

▶ Rich families built large stone memorials over their graves, like these in the Necropolis in Glasgow. In general, the dead were buried, but in the late Victorian period people began to cremate (burn) the bodies.

Some children joined a Christian group called the Band of Hope and 'took the pledge'. This meant that they promised never to drink alcohol even when they were grown up.

The Lord's Day

Sunday was the 'Lord's Day', when people did not do any work at all, and wore their best clothes. Most shops were closed and the streets were very quiet. Children could not run about but had to read religious books or play quietly with special Sunday toys like a model Noah's Ark.

Sunday school

Most children spent a Sunday morning or afternoon at Sunday school, even if their parents didn't go to church. Here they were taught stories from the Bible and sang hymns. Compared to staying at home, Sunday school was often much more fun, with prizes, teas and outings to the countryside or seaside.

◀ A Sunday school class in 1858. For some children, Sunday school was the only school they went to, and it was their only chance of learning to read and write.

Clothing and Fashion

Although cloth was made in the textile mills of the north of England, clothes were made mostly by hand. To buy a new jacket or skirt usually meant a visit to a tailor, who would measure the customer and make clothes specially for him or her.

Victorian clothes were heavy and difficult to wash. Poorer people often had to make do with one set of clothes for work and perhaps another set for Sunday. Life could be smelly on hot days!

▲This large family group, photographed at the end of the 19th century, has been celebrating a wedding. The women's hats are decorated with feathers or flowers, while the men wear dark suits.

Outdoors nearly everyone wore a hat, bonnet or cap. Men wore dull-coloured jackets and shirts. They also wore waistcoats, with a pocket often containing a watch attached to a chain.

What women wore

Among wealthier women the new look in the early years of Victoria's reign was the crinoline. This was a long, wide skirt worn over a large frame made of steel and whalebone hoops. Walking about and sitting down were quite difficult.

WASHING CLOTHES

Monday was traditionally the day for women to do the washing. First the clothes were soaked in hot soapy water. To get the dirt out the clothes were bashed with a wooden device called a 'dolly', or scraped along a ridged washboard. Then they were rinsed and the water was squeezed out between the rollers of a 'mangle'. Later in the week, having been hung out to dry, the clothes were ironed. Before electric irons were invented in 1882 a 'flat iron' was heated up in the fire, or a 'box iron' was filled with hot coals or chunks of hot iron.

After 1875 the crinoline went out of fashion and women began to wear elegant dresses with a bustle – the skirt was padded and bunched up at the back. Rich women followed the latest fashions from Paris, which appeared in magazines.

Black for mourning

A death in the family meant that the relatives were in **mourning** and were expected to wear black clothes for months. If they could not afford new clothes they might have to dye their favourite clothes black.

▼An advertisement from about 1890. Under her dress, a woman wore a whalebone corset to make her waist slim. Victorian women sometimes fainted because their corsets were so tight.

▲An advertisement for boys' clothing. In late Victorian times middle-class children, both boys and girls, were often dressed in sailors' suits. Many wore high boots with long laces. When they were very young both boys and girls wore short dresses. At school, girls wore white pinafores (sleeveless aprons) over their dresses.

After the Victorians

Queen Victoria died in 1901 at Osborne House, her home on the Isle of Wight. Her body was taken by ship and train to London. When it arrived at Victoria Station, huge crowds were waiting in the streets to see the royal coffin. After 64 years the Victorian age had finally come to an end.

By 1901 Britain was no longer the most powerful country in the world. Other countries like the United States and Germany had become very rich too. But for many people, life at the beginning of the 20th century continued very much as it had in the 1890s.

Reminders of the Victorian age

Life has changed in many ways since then. For example, few people in Britain now work as servants or miners. But the Victorians also introduced many new things we now take for granted, such as railways and electric street lighting. Postage stamps are also a Victorian invention, and any postbox with VR on it (standing for *Victoria Regina*, or Queen Victoria) dates from Victorian times.

▲ Everyone dressed in black to watch Queen Victoria's coffin being pulled by horses through London's streets, February 1901.

Many Victorian buildings are still standing. These include houses, museums, railway stations, bridges, seaside piers, town halls, public libraries, churches and schools all around Britain. Victorian architecture is often grand and richly decorated.

VICTORIAN TIMEKEEPING

Before the Victorian period people used the sun or else church bells to guess the approximate time. But the new trains, factories and schools needed to keep to timetables, and so people had to set their clocks and watches exactly. For the first time, clocks began to use exactly the same time across the whole country.

The Victorians also had many ideas that are still important today. They made changes that improved their lives and ours. Clean drinking water was supplied to towns. Laws stopped children working in factories and mines and made them go to school. People began to take more holidays. They also travelled around more, because of improved transport systems such as the railways.

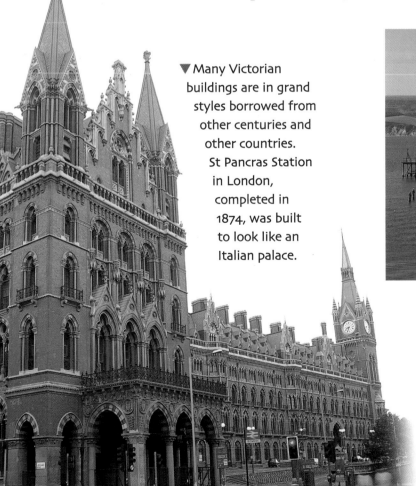

▼ Many Victorian buildings are in grand styles borrowed from other centuries and other countries. St Pancras Station in London, completed in 1874, was built to look like an Italian palace.

▲ This wooden pier in Swanage, in Dorset, was built in 1893, when the town was becoming a busy seaside resort. Many visitors arrived there by train.

Timeline

1819 Birth of Princess Victoria.

1837 Victoria becomes queen of Britain.

1838 First photograph taken.

1840 Queen Victoria marries Albert; first postage stamps introduced.

1851 The Great Exhibition opens in London; first free public library opens in Winchester.

1856 Police forces now in every town.

1861 Prince Albert dies.

1864 A law bans boys under 10 from working as chimney sweeps.

1865 Invention of antiseptics.

1868 Invention of the bicycle.

1870 Schools provided for 5- to 10-year-olds.

1871 Bank Holiday Act introduced, allowing banks to close a few days a year.

1872 First FA Cup Final.

1875 Public Health Act becomes law, allowing councils to demolish slums.

1876 Telephone invented.

1880 Education compulsory for all children.

1895 First motor car factory opens in Birmingham.

1901 Death of Queen Victoria.

Places to Visit

Museum of Childhood at Bethnal Green, London
Toys, dolls' houses, and other mementoes of childhood.

Black Country Living Museum, Dudley, Warwickshire
A reconstructed Victorian village in the industrial Black Country.

Brodsworth Hall, South Yorkshire
One of Britain's best examples of what a great Victorian house was like.

City Chambers, Glasgow
A magnificent 1880s city hall, with marble staircases and huge rooms.

Cragside, near Rothbury, Northumberland
Built in the 1880s, this large house had all the latest inventions, like telephones, a passenger lift, electric light and central heating.

Inveraray Jail, Inveraray, Argyll, Scotland
A museum set in a real 19th-century prison, where you can find out what hard labour was like and what it was like to be locked up in a cell.

Ironbridge Gorge Industrial Museum, Ironbridge, Shropshire
The birthplace of the Industrial Revolution. This museum is on several sites and includes Blists Hill Victorian Village.

Lanhydrock House, near Lostwithiel, Cornwall
A grand house rebuilt in Victorian times.

Museum of Welsh Life, St Fagans, near Cardiff, Wales
Buildings from all over Wales, including some from the Victorian period.

Osborne House, Isle of Wight
A house built for Queen Victoria, and where she died in 1901.

Port Sunlight, Cheshire and **Saltaire, Bradford, West Yorkshire**
Two beautiful Victorian factory villages, where the factory owners built good houses for their workers.

Ragged School Museum, Copperfield Road, London
One of the many ragged schools for poor children, now a museum.

The Workhouse, Southwell, Nottinghamshire
A 19th-century workhouse where homeless and sick people lived, ate and worked.

SS *Great Britain*, Bristol docks, Bristol
The world's first propeller-driven iron ship.

Glossary

chapel a building that is plainer than a church and is used for worship by groups like the Baptists.

commuting travelling to work every day from the suburbs to a city centre.

governess woman who teaches the children of a family and lives in their home.

lower class poorest part of the population.

middle class the part of the population who lived comfortably but were not particularly rich – the man of the house might go to work.

mourning the time after someone has died when mourners wore black to show their respects.

nanny a woman employed by parents to look after their children.

omnibus a bus, pulled by horses, or driven by steam, electricity or petrol.

raw materials products such as wool or iron that need to be processed into other items before they are used.

sewer a tunnel into which dirty water and toilet waste from houses and other buildings flows.

slum a badly built home, often overcrowded and dirty, and perhaps without water supply or proper drainage.

social class a group of people who all have similar backgrounds, wealth and education.

textile mill a factory where cotton or wool was made into cloth.

trade union an organisation that looked after workers, and tried to improve their pay and working conditions.

upper class the richest part of the population, who had big houses and did not usually go to work.

Books and Websites

Books

Karen Bryant-Mole, *My Victorian Home*, Franklin Watts, 1995

Peter Chrisp, *On the Trail of the Victorians in Britain*, Franklin Watts, 1999

John Malam, *The Past in Pictures: The Victorians*, Hodder Wayland, 1999

John Malam, *You Wouldn't Want to be a Victorian Miner!* Hodder Wayland, 2002

Brian Milton, *Let's Discover a Victorian Mill*, Franklin Watts, 2002

Neil Morris, *Life in Victorian Times: Sport and Leisure*, Belitha, 1999

Richard Wood, *A Day in the Life of a Victorian Street Seller*, Hodder Wayland, 1999

Richard Wood, *A Victorian School*, Hodder Wayland, 2002

Richard and Sara Wood, *The Illustrated World of the Victorians*, Hodder Wayland, 2000

Rachel Wright, *Craft Topics: The Victorians*, Franklin Watts, 2001

The Victorians, Dorling Kindersley, 1998

Websites

www.bbc.co.uk/schools/victorians
BBC website on children in Victorian Britain. Written for Key Stage 2.

www.channel4.com/learning/microsites/Q/qca/victorians
What it was like to be a child in Victorian Britain.

www.learningcurve.pro.gov.uk/victorianbritain
Exhibition on Victorian Britain, with activities, timelines and questions.

www.history.powys.org.uk/history/intro/primary.html
Topics on life in mid-Wales in Victorian times.

www.schoolhistory.co.uk/primarylinks/victorian.html
Useful links to sites connected to the Victorians and aimed at primary age children.

Index

architecture 5, 10, 12, 14, 18, 28-29

Baptists 24
Bermondsey 11
Bessemer, Henry 6
bicycles 9
Birmingham 4, 10, 15
Blackpool 21
Bolton 4
Bradford 4, 10
Brighton 9
British Empire 5
Brodsworth Hall 6, 17, 20
buses 9, 14

cars 9
Catholics 24
Charing Cross Hospital 23
children 18-19, 25
Church of England 24
clothes 26-27
country life 5, 13
Crystal Palace 5

Dorset 29

electric light 7, 28
entertainment 20-21

food 13, 17
Forth Railway Bridge 7

Glasgow 4, 12, 15, 25
Great Exhibition 5

Hackney 18
hansom cabs 9
health 13, 22-23
Hill, Rowland 6
holidays 21
hospitals 23
houses 12-13, 14, 15, 16-17

industry 4, 10-11, 19
Isle of Wight 16, 28

Lancashire 11, 19
Leeds 4, 12
libraries 20
Llandudno 21
London 5, 7, 8, 13, 14-15, 18, 19,
    23, 28, 29

Lords cricket ground 21
lower class 5, 12-13, 19, 20

Manchester 4, 10, 15
Manningham Mills 10
Margate 21
Methodists 24
middle class 5, 14, 15, 18, 20

National Union of Railwaymen 11
Necropolis 25
Newcastle 4
Nightingale, Florence 23

office work 11
Osborne House 16, 28

Paddington Station 8
phonographs 7
photographs 6
postage stamps 6, 28
Putney 14

Ragged Schools 19
railways 7, 8, 12, 14, 21, 28, 29
religion 24-25

St Pancras Station 29
St Pancras workhouse 13
Saltaire 12
schools 18-19, 25
servants 16-17
ships 7, 9
South Yorkshire 6, 17, 20
sports 21
steam power 7, 8-9
suburbs 14-15
Swanage 29

Tamar Bridge 7
theatres 20-21
toys 20, 25
trade unions 11
trams 9, 14
typewriters 11

upper class 5, 16-17, 18

Victoria, Queen 4, 28

workhouse 13